This edition first published in 2005 by
Sea-to-Sea Publications
1980 Lookout Drive
North Mankato
Minnesota 56003

ISBN   1-932889-22-1

Printed in China

Library of Congress Control Number: 2004103717

2 4 6 8 9 7 5 3

Published by arrangement with the Watts Publishing Group Ltd, London

Author: J. Bastyra and C. Bradley
Illustrated by Michael Evans
Photography by Howard Allman
Series editor: Paula Borton
Series Designer: Robert Walster

LOOK AND MAKE

COOKING

SEA-TO-SEA

Mankato Collingwood London

Getting ready

Before you start, read the recipe and look at the pictures to make sure you have all the ingredients and equipment you need.

Measure out the ingredients carefully. The oven needs at least 15 minutes to warm up, so don't forget to switch it on.

Be prepared

Don't forget to wash your hands before you start. Be careful with knives. If you have to use a sharp knife ask for help.

Remember to wear oven mitts if you are going to touch anything hot. Ask a grown-up to put dishes in or take them out of the oven for you.

Be extra careful when you cook anything on top of the stove. Remember to turn pan handles to one side.

2

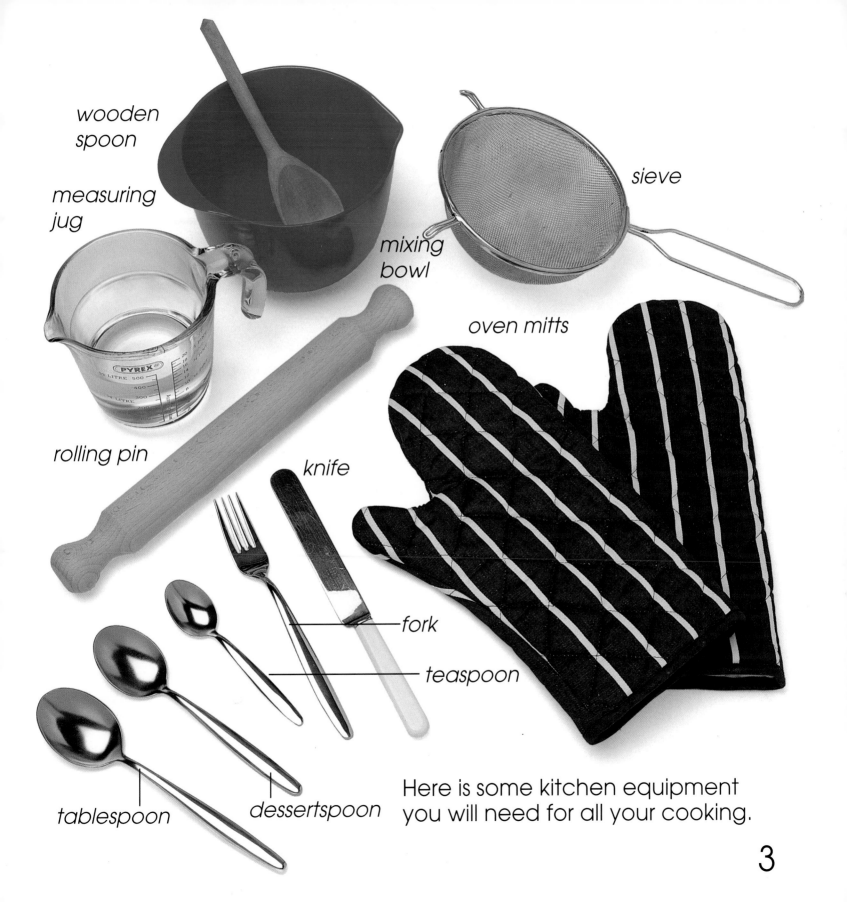

wooden spoon

measuring jug

sieve

mixing bowl

oven mitts

rolling pin

knife

fork

teaspoon

tablespoon

dessertspoon

Here is some kitchen equipment you will need for all your cooking.

3

Jelly turtle

You will need:

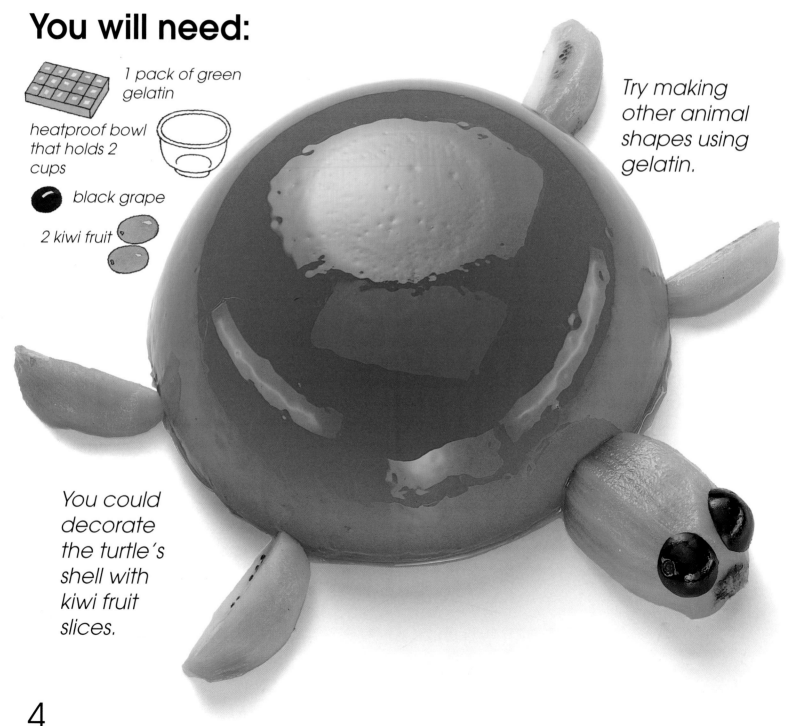

1 pack of green gelatin

heatproof bowl that holds 2 cups

black grape

2 kiwi fruit

Try making other animal shapes using gelatin.

You could decorate the turtle's shell with kiwi fruit slices.

4

1.

Prepare the gelatin following the directions on the pack. Put it in the fridge until set.

2.

Dip the bottom of the bowl into a basin of hot water and run a knife around the edge.

3.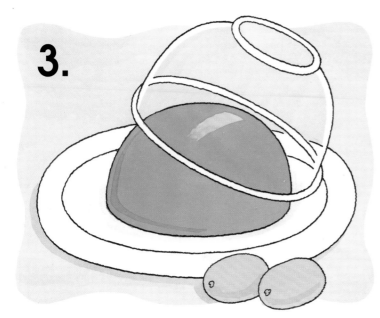

Carefully turn out the gelatin onto a big plate. Ask someone to help. Now peel the kiwi fruit.

4.

Use one kiwi for the head. Cut the other into four for legs. Use half a grape for each eye.

Mallow shapes

You will need:

1 cup
miniature
marshmallows

1 3/4 cups rice
crispies

Before you start
Preheat your oven to
350°F. If you have a
microwave put the
marshmallows with the
rice crispies in a covered
bowl. Microwave for 1-2
minutes on medium.

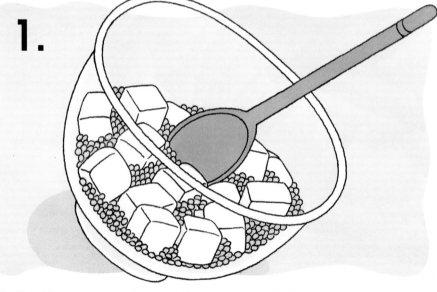

1.

Mix the marshmallows and rice crispies
in an ovenproof bowl. Put it in the oven
for about 20 minutes.

2.

Wearing oven mitts, take
the bowl out of the oven
and place it on a cloth.

Decorate your shapes with candies.

You can make any shape you like. Try copying these ducks.

3.

Mix the crispies and melted marshmallows with a wooden spoon.

4.

Before the mixture gets hard, make shapes by pushing the mixture into cookie cutters or form your own shapes.

Potato heads

Before you start
Preheat your oven to 375°F.
If you have a microwave, wrap the potatoes in paper towels and cook on high for ten minutes

You will need:

2 large potatoes

1/3 cup tuna fish

2 tbsp sweetcorn

2 tbsp butter

baby carrots

baby sweetcorn

salt and pepper

cherry tomatoes

1.

Scrub the potatoes and prick them with a fork. Bake them for 45 minutes.

2.

Cut the potatoes in half longways. Scoop out the soft insides into a bowl. Mix in the tuna, corn, butter, and salt and pepper.

8

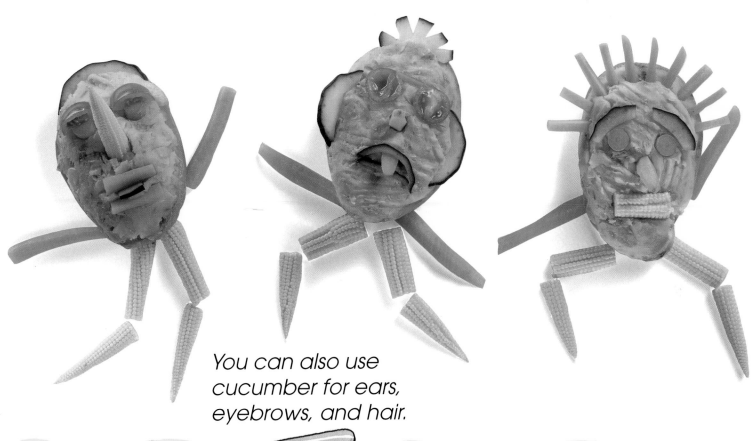

You can also use cucumber for ears, eyebrows, and hair.

3.

Stuff the mixture back into the potato skins and smooth it with the back of a spoon.

4.

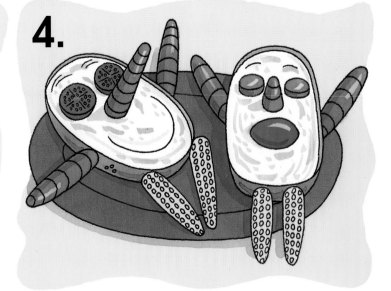

Put the potatoes on plates, and make faces, legs, and arms with vegetables.

9

Rainbow slush

You will need:

orange juice

blackcurrant cordial

lime or strawberry cordial

ice cube trays

This slushy ice is delicious on a hot day. You can make these slushes any flavor you like.
If you don't have any ice cube trays, use shallow plastic dishes.

You can make your slushes any flavor or color you like.

10

1.

Pour the juices into three ice cube trays. Use one tray for each color.

2.

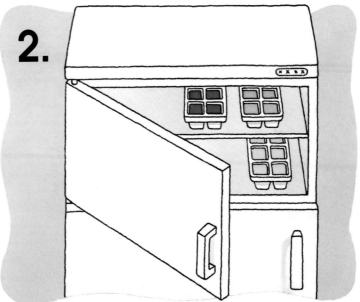

Put the trays in the freezer for about 2-2$\frac{1}{2}$ hours.

3.

Take the trays out and drop the cubes from one tray into a jug. Mash the ice with a fork.

4.

Pour the slush into glasses. Do the same with the other two flavors to make three layers.

11

Giant cookie

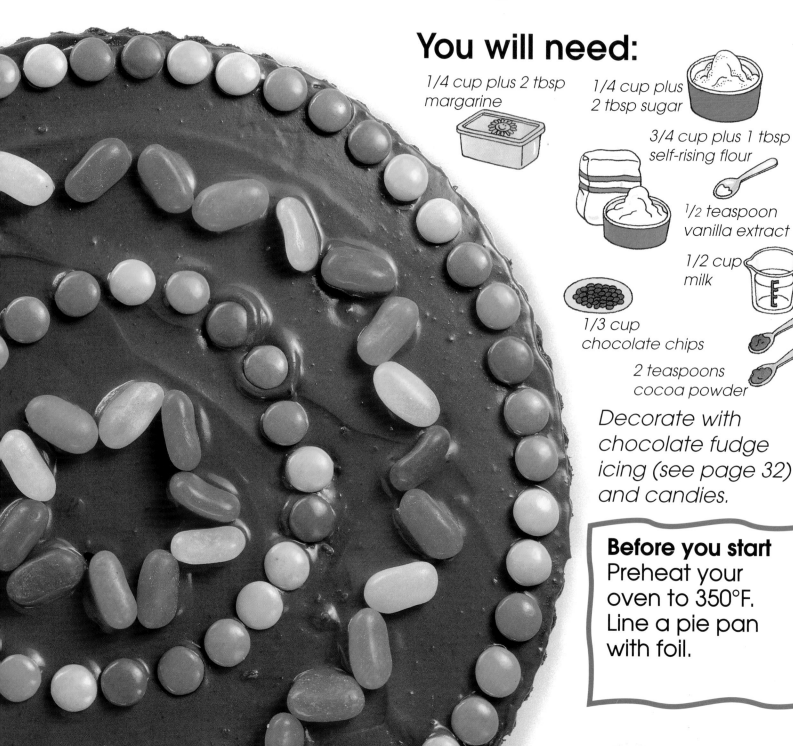

You will need:

1/4 cup plus 2 tbsp margarine

1/4 cup plus 2 tbsp sugar

3/4 cup plus 1 tbsp self-rising flour

1/2 teaspoon vanilla extract

1/2 cup milk

1/3 cup chocolate chips

2 teaspoons cocoa powder

Decorate with chocolate fudge icing (see page 32) and candies.

Before you start
Preheat your oven to 350°F. Line a pie pan with foil.

1.

Mix the margarine and sugar together in a bowl until light and fluffy.

2.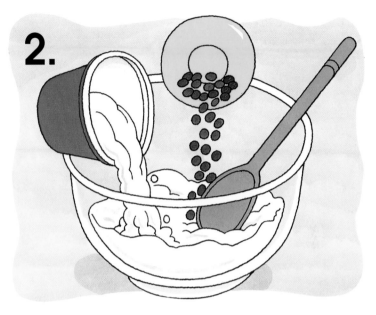

Slowly stir in the flour, then add the chocolate. Use a wooden spoon to mix.

3.

Mix in the vanilla extract, cocoa, and milk.

4.

Spread the mixture into the pie pan. Bake for 25 minutes.

Monster cake

You will need:

2 medium eggs

1/2 cup margarine or butter

candies

3/4 cup plus 1 tbsp self-rising flour

1/2 cup sugar

butter cream icing (see page 19). Make some green and some yellow. Leave a little bit white.

1 teaspoon vanilla extract

paper bake cups

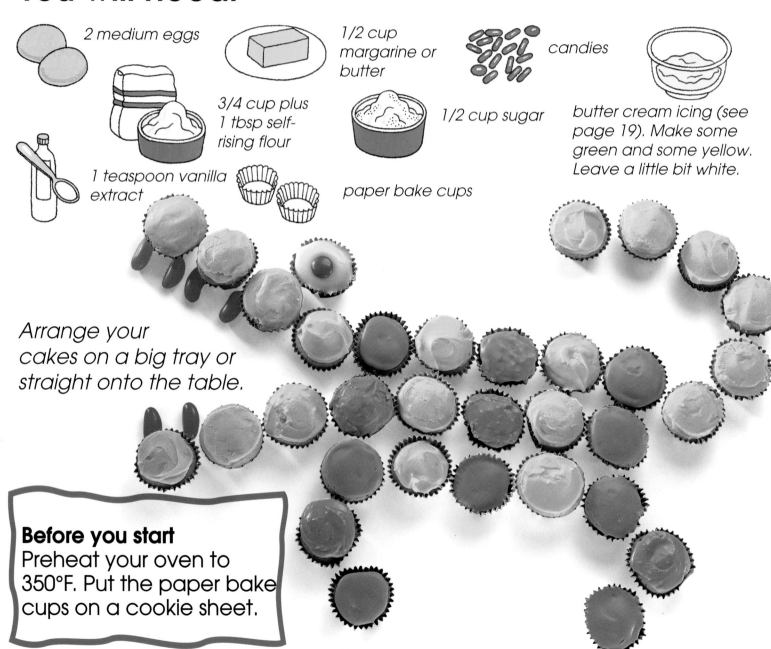

Arrange your cakes on a big tray or straight onto the table.

Before you start
Preheat your oven to 350°F. Put the paper bake cups on a cookie sheet.

1.

Mix the butter and sugar until it is all light and fluffy.

2.

Add the eggs and flour and beat it all until it is smooth. Add the vanilla.

3.

Drop teaspoons of mixture into the cups and bake for about 12 minutes. Cool on a wire rack.

4.

Ice the cakes yellow and green. Make one white. Arrange them as shown here. Add the candies.

Surprise bread

You will need:

1lb all-purpose flour plus a bit extra

1 1/2 cups hot water

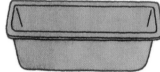

1-lb loaf pan

1 sachet of active dry yeast

1 teaspoon oil

4oz (125g) semisweet or milk chocolate, broken into pieces

1 teaspoon milk

Before you start
Oil the loaf pan to stop your bread from sticking.
Preheat your oven to 400°F.

16

1.

Sift the flour into a bowl and sprinkle on the yeast.

2.

Mix in the hot water and oil to make a dough ball.

3.

Sprinkle flour onto a surface and knead the dough on it by pushing and pulling it with your hands.

4.

Put the dough in a clean bowl. Cover it and leave it to rise for an hour.

5.

Then put half the dough into the pan and scatter on the chocolate.

6.

Add the rest of the dough and brush the top with milk. Bake for 30-35 minutes.

17

Cookie faces

You will need:

Glacé icing

1 cup confectioner's sugar

2 tablespoons water

food coloring*

plain cookies

Butter cream icing

1/4 cup butter or margarine

2 cups confectioner's sugar

1 tablespoon milk

candies for decoration

Make lots of funny faces.

Glacé icing

1.

Sift the sugar into a bowl. Stir in the water.

2.

Mix the coloring in a few drops at a time.

Butter cream icing

1.

Soften the butter by mixing it with a wooden spoon.

2.

Sift in the sugar and then carefully stir it in.

3.

Add the milk and stir in a color or flavor (see the box below).

Decorating

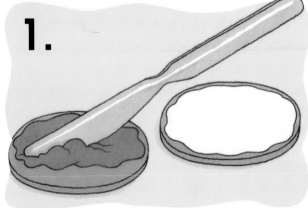

1.

Spread the icing on the cookies. Dip your knife into water after every spread. This makes the job easier.

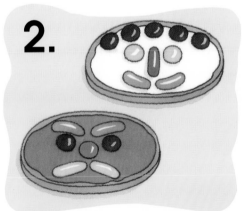

2.

Leave the icing to set for a few minutes, then add the decorations.

Flavor or color butter cream icing by adding lemon, cocoa powder, or melted chocolate.

You can buy natural food coloring in health food stores.

Pasta house

Use celery sticks for trees.

Make your house on a foil-covered cookie sheet.

You will need:

8oz (250 g) pasta twists in three colors

celery

strips of cucumber for window frames

1/4 cup olive oil

1 tablespoon wine vinegar

cherry tomatoes

cheese slices

salt and pepper

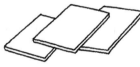

1 teaspoon sugar

20

1.

Ask an adult to boil the pasta shapes in salted water for about 8 minutes for you.

2.

Mix the sugar, salt, pepper, and vinegar in a jug. Slowly add the olive oil, beating with a fork.

3.

Ask an adult to drain the pasta and put it in a bowl. Pour on the dressing and let the pasta cool.

4.

Make your house. Start with the frame and then fill in. Use cheese for the door and windows.

Toffee date dessert

You will need:

5oz (125g) sugared chopped dates—soak them in hot water for an hour

1 1/8 cups sugar

2 tbsp butter

2 eggs

pinch of salt

1/4 teaspoon baking soda

4 teaspoons of baking powder

1 2/3 cups self-rising flour

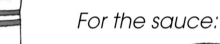

For the sauce:

1/4 cup butter

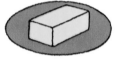

1/3 cup dark brown sugar

1/2 cup light corn syrup

Let the dessert cool a little before you eat it as it is very hot.

1.

Mix the sugar, eggs, butter, salt, flour, baking powder, and baking soda together until it looks like crumbs.

2.

Strain the soaked dates and add. Spoon the mixture into an ovenproof dish and bake for 45 minutes.

3.

Ask an adult for help.

Make the sauce. Put the butter, sugar, and syrup into a saucepan. Cook over a low heat until the sugar has dissolved.

4.

Take the dessert out of the oven and pour the sauce over it.

Pizza snake

You will need:

1 egg

1 tablespoon of olive oil

2 teaspoons active dry yeast

2 cups all-purpose flour

1 teaspoon salt

black olives

cheese slices

1 teaspoon dried oregano or basil

green bell pepper for the snake's tongue

5 tablespoons chopped canned tomatoes (drained of juice)

1/2 cup hot water

Before you start
Preheat your oven to 375°F. Oil a cookie sheet.

1.

Mix the flour, salt, and yeast in a large bowl.

2.

Mix in the egg, oil, and hot water to make a dough.

3.

Knead the dough for five minutes (see page 17).

4.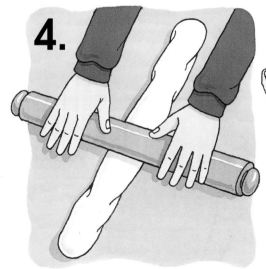

Leave the dough covered in a warm place for an hour. Roll it into a snake.

5.

Curl the snake on a baking sheet. Add tomatoes, herbs, and cheese.

6.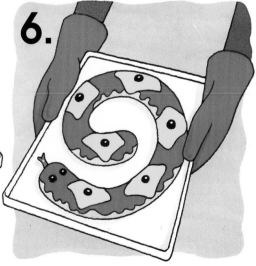

Bake for 15 to 20 minutes. Then add the olives and a green bell pepper tongue.

Popchoc treats

You will need:

2 1/2 cups
plain popcorn

1 tablespoon
of water

2 chocolate-covered
caramel bars

3oz (75g) mixed
fruit and nuts

1.

Chop up the caramel bars.
Put them in a saucepan
with the water.

2.

Ask an adult for help.

Put the saucepan over a low heat
and stir until the chocolate pieces
have melted.

3.

Take the saucepan off the
heat and stir in the fruit and
nuts.

4.

Stir in the popcorn so it is
well coated with chocolate.
Let it cool a little.

5.

Form little balls
with your hands.

*You can leave
out the nuts
if you don't
like them.*

*Add glacé cherries
if you like.*

Jam tarts

You will need:

3/4 cup plus 1 tbsp all-purpose flour plus extra flour for rolling

pinch of salt

1 dessertspoon of sugar

1/2 cup margarine or butter

jam

pastry cutter

tartlet pans

2 tablespoons iced water

Before you start
Preheat your oven to 350°F. Grease the pans with a little butter.

You can add pastry shapes to your tarts.

1.

Sift the flour and salt into a bowl. Cut the butter into pieces and add it in.

2.

Rub the butter into the flour until it looks like crumbs.

3.

Add the sugar and stir in the water. Mix it into a dough.

4.

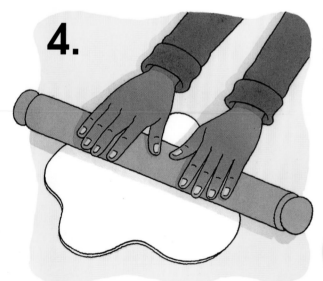

Sprinkle some flour onto a surface and roll out the pastry. It should be about 1/4 in (5mm) thick.

5.

Cut out rounds of pastry and lay them in the pans. Put a teaspoon of jam into each one.

6.

Bake for about 15 minutes, or until the pastry is golden brown.

Magic marble cake

You will need:

1 2/3 cups self-rising flour (sieved)

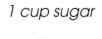
1 cup sugar

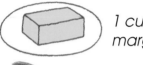
1 cup butter or margarine

1 teaspoon vanilla extract

1 tablespoon cocoa powder (sieved)

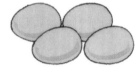
9-inch (23-cm) cake pan

1/2 teaspoon pink food coloring*

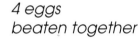
4 eggs beaten together

Decorate with choc fudge icing. See page 32 for how to make it.

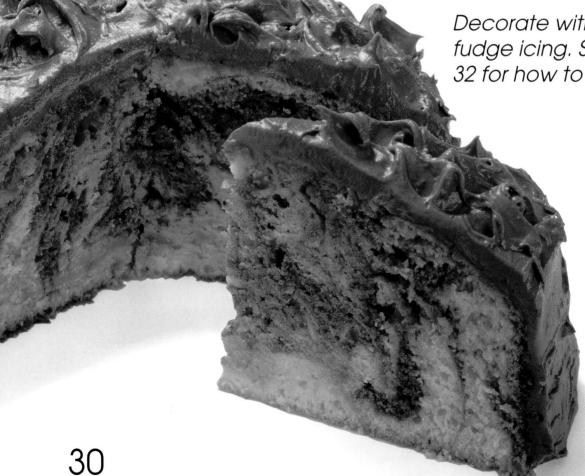

Before you start
Preheat your oven to 350°. Grease your cake pan with some butter. Then sprinkle in a little flour and shake it. This will stop the cake from sticking.

1.

Beat the butter and sugar together until fluffy. Stir in the eggs and flour.

2.

Divide the mixture into three. Add vanilla to one bowl. Add pink coloring to another and cocoa to the third.

3.

Spoon the mixture into the pan, taking turns with each color. Swirl the colors just once to make a marble pattern.

4.

Bake for 40-45 minutes. Leave to cool for a few minutes, then turn it out onto a rack.

* You can buy natural food coloring in health food stores.

Choc fudge icing

You will need:

1/2 cup sugar

1/2 cup milk

1/4 cup butter or margarine

6oz (150g) semisweet chocolate, broken into small pieces.

1.

Melt the sugar with the milk over a low heat. Ask a grown-up to help.

2.

Bring to a boil, then simmer for two minutes.

3.

Take the saucepan off the heat and stir in the chocolate and butter.

4.

Cook the mixture for another minute and keep stirring. Leave it to cool and thicken before spreading.

Index